Poetry to God

Volume 2

NO FAULT FOUND

TERRY WEBB

Printed in the United States of America.

ISBN: 978-0-6157-3306-7

Library of Congress Control Number: 2011901030

To my father God:

I thank you my Heavenly Father,
For keeping me focused and giving
me strengh to follow my dreams as a poet/writer.
I thank you for your spirit and character showing me the way.
I am forever grateful.

I am grateful for my imagination. I will be open to having
faith in all possibilities.

I am grateful being a part of your creation and being chosen
to write your book *"POETRY TO GOD Volume 2"*

SPECIAL DEDICATION

Special Thanks: To **Jermaine M. Harris** "Executive director" of Black Family United, **Azaan Kamau** "Executive director" of Glover Lane Press, **Regina Fair** "Executive director" of Fair Opportunity For Change Inc. and to L. A Talk Radio Host **Audrey Liggens of Ms. Audreys House** for all the help and support they have given me with my first published book, "POETRY TO GOD"Volume 1 . . . . I am forever grateful.

A Very Special Thanks: To all my family, To Sheriff Clergy **Gerald Murphy Sr.** To Sheriff Clergy **Rev. D. L. Goree,** To the L. A. County Sheriff Department, To my Supervisors and all my co workers at General Discount, But mostly to all my loyal friends and readers who have so kindly and vigorously supported and encouraged me in my writing journey. I am gratefully indebted for all your efforts.

Most People Have one Church home, but I have "3"
And A Very Special Thanks To all the congregation of brothers and sisters at all 3 Church's

CITY OF REFUGE: Bishop Noel Jones,
Minister Edwin Perry, Deacon Edwards, Demetrius Edwards, Deacon Joe Lewis Cobb, Deacon Ted Irby, Deacon Al Kimbell, Deacon Clifford Brown, Ricky Cole, Willie Rosas, Kesha Tucker, Shakarra Ross, Velma Moss, Jerry Butler, Davion Mines, Rose Marie Waters, Joann Swim, Jackie Swim, David Mikes, Prentis Hill, Teddy Williams, Sister Witherspoon, Brother & Sister Eric Clay, Linda Winfield, Janta Rice Gwen Kinnard, Sondra Blue, Marilyn Wells, Tonya Jackson, Charles Earls, Roy Ross, Davion Jones, Lionel Witherspoon, Sheila Manning, Maryann Madison, Morris White, Evangelist Grace Darling, and Mama Grahm . . . . I Love you Mama Grahm :-)

SPECIAL DEDICATION CONTINUED

NEW MOUNT CALVARY: Pastor Sonja Dawson,
My Bible Study Group: Deacon Donald Harris, Allen Stewart, Alma Johnson, Charles and Nancy Moore, Alta Jones, Deborah Houston Wong, Gala Houston Allen, Carolyn Houston Flicklin, Barbera Causey, Glendarice Palacio, Rhonda Richard, Pamela Hodges, Norman Anderson, Donna Jackson, Marlisa Allen, Manette Wesley, Paulett Kendrick, Lomila Martin, Carol Ferns, Kathy Browder, Wilbert Allen, Saraya Potts and Bridgette Hale

CALVARY RESURRECTIONAL: Pastor Scipio Stubbs Jr.
Sister Stubbs "The first lady" and family, Mother Worline and family, Rev. Joey Seals and family, The Mosely family, Deacon Robert Webb and family, Deacon Stansbury and family, The Parker family, The Mitchel family, The White family, The Miller family, Deacon Walker and family, The Armstrong family, The Harris family, The Deguzman family and The Harrison family

May God bless you all and I truly thank God for all of you being a part of my life . . .

Sincerely Yours
TERRY WEBB

FORWORD

For the readers of "POETRY TO GOD" by Terry Webb, this book is the second volume of Spiritual Inspirational Poetry in a series of 4 Volumes. This book is also as motivating and inspiring as was the first. In this book, you'll find beautifully illustrated poems that will help you in your everyday walk of life with yourself and with God. In this book you'll also find that faith helps you deal with the stormy challenges of life, abuses, and relationships. The poems in this book are as powerful as the ones in the first book, "POETRY TO GOD volume 1" and they're intended to keep your mind and heart focused on the things of God. I recommend this book to all readers wanting a closer walk with God. Remember that without change, there's no growth.

Terry Webb

CONTENTS

"NO FAULT FOUND"

He was whipped, kicked, and spit upon
He was despised and rejected by men,
He was bruised for our iniquities
Yet, this man, He never knew sin!
But the sins of this world were upon Him
And His head He held up high,
He took the place of all mankind
Sentenced, now to die!
A crown of thorns, they placed on Him
They nailed His hands and feet,
Upon a cross, on Calvary's hill
In blazing desert heat.
He never uttered a word at all–
Although He was facing death,
He endured the hurting, agonizing pain
Till His very last of breath.
"My God, why hast Thou forsaken me?"
Were the only words that He cried,
One of the soldiers that was standing by
Then pierced him in his side.
Blood and water came out of Him
Spilling upon the ground,
His life was given for all mankind
Yet no fault in Him was found!

By Terry Webb

"NEVER ENDING STORY"

Please open up your heart and mind
And listen to this story,
How the son of God had left His home
In Heavens mighty glory.

As a child He came to earth
To be born in a manger,
The earth and man He made His own
Man thought of Him a stranger.

He made His home with all mankind
But what did mankind do?
They rejected and they crucified
The Lord whom was so true.

He emptied all Himself, but love
For all the human race,
Though it was man who shed His blood
He extends to man His grace.

For by His blood, in which was shed
Our sin's are fully paid,
For when they nailed Him on that cross
Our sin's, on Him were laid.

He took the place of all mankind
Leaving all His glory,
Through the years mankind has told
This never ending story.

By Terry Webb

"FORMED BY GOD"

I never gave a second thought
How long my life would last–
I never thought where I was going
When my life was past.

My life was broken into two
Time and time again–
Shattered by the way I lived
Deeply into sin.

In sin, I did not understand
But now I've come to see–
That through my life of hurt and pain
You were shaping me.

Forming me to what I am
A beauty never known–
Although the life I lived was marred
Your love was clearly shown,

For you, "O" Lord have touched my life
In many different ways–
You formed my life to what I am
For this I give You Praise,

By: TERRY WEBB

"ALL I NEED"

All I need is someone who care-
To keep me from all harm,
I need someone to protect me from-
The devils awful charm.

I need this person to always be there-
Always by my side,
To walk with me and talk with me-
Sometimes to give me a ride.

I need someone for sometimes I fall-
And I'm unable to follow through,
To pick me up and carry me-
And help in things I do.

I need the Lord Jesus Christ-
He is my all in all,
For he has been the only one-
To answer when I call.

Written by: Terry Webb

"A WONDERFUL SAVIOR"

Oh what a wonderful Savior Thou Art,
Whom knows the troubles of our heart.
He knows our spirit and inner soul,
He has the power, He has control.
He leads the path of life each day,
He'll carry you, when you fall from the way.
Full of mercy, with a tender touch,
With a heart of love, even as much.
He is salvation, this Lord above,
A wonderful Savior, Jesus is love.

By Terry Webb

"FAITH"

Faith is the substance we hope for and
The evidence of things unseen,
Purge your mind and heart with God
Your path will then be seen.

It's better to walk with God by faith–
Than go alone by sight,
Those who look in faith to Him–
Their steps He'll lead upright.

We need the faith of little children–
Just as a child possess,
Just as a little child in God–
In their innocence.

We need that childlike faith in God–
Innocent and trustingly,
That never will falter and never fail–
That's how our faith should be.

So keep thy feet upon His path–
And do not ask to see,
The distant scene of life prepared–
In faith, "let God's will be!"

By Terry Webb

"A FRIEND OF JESUS"

You are my friends, if you do what I say,
You are my friends, if only you'll pray.
You are my friends, if only you'll start,
Giving your love, and opening your heart.

You are my friends, if you love one another,
Sharing your love, and loving your brother.
You are my friends, if you except my love,
That I pour down to you, from Heaven above.

By Terry Webb

"BEING GRACIOUS"

The grace of God, has appeared to all men-
Being generous, though man live in sin,
He show a gracious spirit, with forgiveness-
Although man do not deserve, such kindness.

Not giving punishment, to man whom deserve-
The punishment of God, is now on reserve,
God extends his hand, He is so generous-
God's mercy and grace, towards all of us.

By: TERRY WEBB

"A CHOSEN FEW"

Many are called, but few are chosen
Who shall enter His rest?
Not many wise, the Lord has chosen
But some, they are blest.

We try and try to live our lives
the best way as we can,
But we don't live accordingly
To Gods eternal plan.

"O" Lord, when You return for us
Reveal, "O" Lord, Thy grace,
For showing love that's not deserved
From me, turn not Thy face.

By Terry Webb

"CHOSEN TO SHINE"

Like stars we are to shine-
Unto God's Holy face,
As He looks upon from Heaven-
On the human race.
Chosen we are His children-
Transformed from a life,
A life inside of darkness-
And frightful, painful strife.
We are to shine like stars-
That illuminate the darkness,
For the sake of those still living-
In dark bitterness.
Shine people shine-
Throughout the night and day,
To overcome the darkness-
In a graceful way.
Shine people shine-
You chosen children of God,
Let your light shine brightly-
On every road you trod.

By: TERRY WEBB

"CHOSEN TO SUFFER"

Man will have troubles, on each road that he trod-
But he must stand firm, and seek the face of God,
Trials and tribulations, we all must go through-
It's God's special process, made complete in you,
He does not want man, to fear suffering-
Only to endure, the painful trial it brings,
Christ suffered so, we must also share-
The pain and the suffering, we must also bear,
We are chosen to suffer, in some tribulation-
Only to reign, in God's Holy nation.

By: TERRY WEBB

"AIM A LIFE FOR HEAVEN"

Each man has a goal in life, to make reality,
He want to be successful, in what he wants to be.
He aims his life well, but he aims the wrong way,
Wanting earthly positions, placing Christ out his way.
We should aim for Heaven, only then we will grow,
We will grow in all things, everywhere we go.
Not lusting in this world, for earthly valued treasures,
Or traipsing through our life, lusting for it's pleasures.
Aim a life for Heaven, seek the Kingdom of God,
God will surely guide you, on every road you trod.
Seek and live your life with God, and he will add to you,
A truly rewarding life, in all things you do.

By Terry Webb

A TOUGH LOVE

Gods love is not permissive, for you it's demanding,
He is a God of love, also understanding.
He disciplines those He love, and place them in His care,
No matter where you go in life, He also will be there.

For God has chosen you, now also he will bruise you,
For you to live for Him, in all things you do.
Gods disciplining love, has a little sting of pain,
Teaching right from wrong, so in life you may gain.

Gods disciplining love, will also help you see,
His disciplining love, will also set you free.
Gods disciplining love, is unforgettable,
His disciplining love, is indispensable.

"God is Love "Always

Written by: Terry Webb

"BE TRUE"

The Lord He said to me one day–
To dwell amongst the just,
He said to me, to trust in Him–
And make His name my trust.
He said to me, to spread His Word–
My witness, will ring true,
Above all, to live for Him–
In all I say and do . . .

By: TERRY WEBB

"BE STRONG"

Be strong and courageous, don't be terrified,
The Lord will be with you, yes, He will provide.
He will enable you to do, His perfect will,
Glorious Lord above, He made peace be still.
The Lord will always be, side by side with you,
Don't be discouraged, He will see you through.

By Terry Webb

"BY GRACE"

By Grace. one day the Lord He came–
And shed His blood for me,
By Grace, one day He gave His life–
That I should be set free.

By Grace, He died then took the keys–
Of death that had me bound,
By Grace, He rose to the side of God–
There His grace is found.

By Terry Webb

"SAFE IN THIS HANDS"

Come to me, my troubled child–
Bring all thy cares to me,
Into my hands, lay all thy fears–
So I may comfort thee.
Bring all thy cares and worries child–
Unto my Holy throne,
That I may wipe away thy tears–
"O" child you are mine own.
So trust in me, "O" troubled child–
To save thee from alarm,
For I, Jesus Christ the Lord–
Will keep thee from all harm.

Written by: Terry Webb

"CREATION"

Oh the beauty of God's creations–
Beyond what you have known,
From the forest green to the mountains peak–
God's handy work is shown.

The cloudy sky's and the stars above–
The gulf that God did span,
Even the greatest of all creation–
God's creation of Man!

By: TERRY WEBB

"FOREVER FRIENDS"

Lord, help me be a friend, true to someone today,
Help me be a special friend, to help in every way.
Lord, take away distrust, and also jealousy,
Help me be a loving friend, make this out of me.

Lord, I want to be your friend, yielded to God's will,
Help me be this kind of friend, always to fulfill.
Lord, lets be friends forever, through all eternity,
Lets be friends always, together You and me.

By Terry Webb

FOREVER NEAR

Wonderfully shining, gleaming bright,
The Lord gives man his radiant light.
High in the Heaven's skies above,
The Lord sends man His thoughtful love.
Shining bright, His love so dear,
The Lord is always forever near.
Above the Heaven's starry skies,
He looks upon man with loving eyes.

By Terry Webb

"FORGIVE TO BE FORGIVEN"

To be forgiven, first learn how to forgive,
It's the way of Jesus, It's the way to live.
Brotherly love, is so important you see,
Jesus forgave us all, this is the way to be.
With a kind and loving heart, that endures to the end,
Not with a deceitful heart, corruptly filled with sin.
Jesus is an example, He forgave all who came,
To Him each one is equal, and sinfully the same.
So learn the ways of Jesus, love your brother and give,
Your heart pure with love, and willing to forgive.

By Terry Webb

"FRIENDS"

A friend is someone good to have, and very important too,
A friend will be there by your side, to help in things you do.
A true friend will teach and help, his friend how to pray,
A friend will teach and help, his friend to live each day.
A friend will help a friend, in a given time of need,
A friend will make a friend, stop and then take heed.
A friend is very special, to the one he calls his friend,
A friends love will endure, until the very end.
Jesus is my friend, and He wants to be yours too,
He will guide you always, He will lead you through.
But nevertheless here I am, I'll be your friend too,
I will help when you need, cause I'm a friend to you!

By Terry Webb

"GAIN THROUGH PAIN"

Throughout our lives of ups and downs–
God sends us joy through pain,
Through all our grief, through bitter loss–
For our greatest gain.

Through it all, God has in hand–
Our days, both dark and bright,
It is His way of shaping lives–
To be both true and right.

By: TERRY WEBB

"HE DIED FOR SIN"

Jesus Christ, He left His throne
In Heaven's glorious sky,
He left His throne to come to earth
For sin, He came to die.

The Lord, He came to show this world
On how each one must live,
He taught us all, how we must love
And how to share and give.

He came to guide and lead the way
To Heaven high above,
He left His home to come to earth
He did this out of love.

He left His Heavenly Host of Angels
Seated there on High,
For sin, He came to give His life
For both you and I.

From Heaven, He came down to us
To die within our place,
To show a dying world His love
And magnify His grace.

In the light of His glory and grace
He gave His life for sin,
To cleanse our hearts, with His own blood
That He may dwell within.

By Terry Webb

"HEAVENS WAY"

I live my life,
Day by day,
I let the Lord,
Lead my way.
He leads me in,
Righteousness,
Through a world,
Such as this.
I walk through,
This life of sin,
Knowing one day,
All sin will end.
I journey up,
The small thin road,
With Jesus helping,
Carry my load.
It's very hard,
But day by day,
I'm a little closer,
To Heaven's way.

By Terry Webb

"THE B.I.B.L.E."

Through the pages of this given book
May we behold from day to day,
God's Basic Instruction Before Leaving Earth
New light to guide our way.
It holds the key to a happy life
Through it's pages, if we look,
Blessed is the Word of God
Written inside this Book.

By Terry Webb

OCEAN TIDE POOL

Tides come in, and tides go out,
Every twenty four hours no doubt.
Bringing in life and later coming for it again,
Somewhat the same as Jesus and man.

Man has his life, then puts it down,
To run through this world, round and round.
But later in life, he find he can't win,
So he turn to Jesus, to be picked up again.

Tides come and tides go,
To watch the waves is a classic show.
Man go up and man go down,
Through this world, round and round.

Written by: Terry Webb

"ONE STEP MORE"

A hill is not to hard to climb,
If you take one step at a time.
One step is not to hard to take,
One try is not to much to make.
One step, two steps, will turn to three,
"Jesus said," Come follow me.
Each step you make, the Lord makes two,
Every step you take, He is there with you.
One try, one step, one song, one smile,
Will help your walk, mile after mile.
Press forward, your prize is life,
From earthly sorrow and bitter strife.
To reach the crown of life your score,
Take one step more, and one step more.

By Terry Webb

"THE LORD OUR SHEPARD"

The Lord is our Sheppard–
And we are His sheep,
Day thru night protecting us–
Without a wink of sleep.

He assembles us together–
High upon a hill,
He feeds us from His own hand–
While He makes peace be still.

The Lord is our Sheppard–
Let's lift our voice and sing,
Songs of joyous praise–
To our Lord and King.

Let's bow to Him in worship–
Let's pray on bending knee,
To our Lord and Savior–
The One who set us free.

By Terry Webb

"THE LORD IS JUDGE"

Why do we judge our fellowman-
but look not at our sin,
Consider the plank in your own eye-
Who made you a judge of men?

Forgive him as the Lord did you-
And do each day God's will,
the Lord is judge and Him alone-
Just trust and serve Him still.

By Terry Webb

"PRESS FOWARD!"

Fear not my child, press forward
Although thy trials be near,
For I, the Lord will be with you
So who then shall you fear.
My staff will always comfort you
I'll guard you with my rod,
So there, my child press forward
And trust in Me Your God.

Written By: Terry Webb

"GOD HEARS OUR CRY"

Through out each day, the Lord will do
And what He do is well,
What is great and what is small
The Lord alone can tell.
For when you kneel before Him
Your heart He truly knows,
Words which can't be uttered find
God's Holy sweet repose.
God will grant you faith to see
That he alone control,
Even in life when you are weak
And falter in your soul.
The Lord Thy God will help you live
Your life in such a way,
You'll cast your love and care on Him
When you unfold and pray.
For when you pray, God hears your cry
When you reach to Him in prayer,
Your love for God should always move
Showing God you care.
The Lord Thy God He sees thy works
As it were greatest of all,
Nothing is lost that's done for God
Even if it's small.
The Lord Thy God will comfort you
And all thy needs supply,
God offers relief and strength to endure
God, He hears our cry.

By Terry Webb

"HOLD MY HAND"

Through the valley of the shadow of death
In death's dark vale of shade,
My hand will guide and lead you through
My child be not afraid.

Trust me child and hold my hand
For I will lead thy soul,
Thy life, think not of future plans
Give me complete control.

My rod and staff shall comfort thee
You need not doubt or fear,
My hand will always hold you child
For I am always near.

Just trust and hold my hand and see
Where I will leadeth thee,
Trust and hold my hand my child
With faith implicitly.

My child believe and trust in Me
For I will make thee stand,
By the power of my wisdom and might
My child, hold my hand.

By Terry Webb

"HE DIED FOR SIN!"

Jesus Christ, He left His throne
In Heaven's glorious sky,
He left His throne to come to earth
For sin, He came to die.

The Lord, He came to show this world
On how each one must live,
He taught us all, how we must love
And how to share and give.

He came to guide and lead the way
To Heaven high above,
He left His home to come to earth
He did this out of love.

He left his Heavenly Host of Angels
Seated there on high,
For sin, He came to give His life
For both you and I.

From Heaven, He came down to us
To die within our place,
To show a dying world His love
And magnify His grace.

In the light of His glory And grace
He gave His life for sin,
To cleanse our hearts, with His own blood
That He may dwell within.

Written By: Terry Webb

"HE DIED FOR ALL"

When I think of all the pain our Lord
On Calvary, He did bear,
For all the sins of all mankind
He hung and suffered there.

His Life was for the price of sin
Which nothing else could buy,
What more can we now ask of him?
He took our place to die.

Written By: Terry Webb

"HOW CAN IT BE"

How can it be, although in sin-
God's loving grace, is on all men,
How can it be, God gave his son-
To a world corrupt, since it begun.

How can it be, that Jesus Christ-
Gave his life, to pay sins price,
How can it be, though all were lost-
His life has paid, for all sins cost.

How can it be, He extends his hand-
And gives his love, to the sinful man,
How can it be, he prepared a place-
for every man, in the human race.

How can it be, He has such heart-
To have this love, that never part,
How can it be, in this sinful world-
He loves every man, woman, boy and girl.

How can it be, He is so true-
To have such love, for me and you,
How can it be, I don't understand-
This type of love, God has for man.

By: Terry Webb

"PARENTS 10 COMMANDMENTS"

1. Teach them using the word of God
Teach them what to do,

2. Teach them what is right and wrong
You must set an example too.

3. See your children as gifts from God
Given by God's own hand,

4. And guide them always in Godly ways
It's what the Lord demand.

5. An important law of God do say
Discipline your loving child,

6. And to love them unconditionally
All their life long while.

7. Parents, do not provoke them to wrath
But fill love within their heart,

8. Then teach them to respect the Lord
That their love for them not part.

9. You must provide for their physical needs
Responsibility shows you care,

10. And then pass your faith along to them
Then to their children they will share.

By: Terry Webb

"TEARDROPS FROM HEAVEN"

From life's grief, hurt, sorrow and pain,
Heaven opens up her showers of rain.
Its like a tear from ones crying eyes,
The same as the rain falling from the skies.
Tears of pain from a person who's hurt,
Tears of rain washing away polluted dirt.
Tears of pain and tears of rain,
To me are somewhat basically the same.
Dripitty drop, dripitty drop,
Tears of pain please come to a stop.
Dripitty drop, dripitty drop,
Tears of rain will you also stop.
From life's grief, hurt sorrow and pain,
Heaven opens up her showers of rain.

By: Terry Webb

"THE LIGHT"

Each day that come, it giveth light,
That turns the darkness, from the night.
that bringeth light, to each new day,
to guide each man, along his way.
Though day's are dim, the light is bright,
Jesus Christ, He is the light.

By: Terry Webb

"TRUE COMFORT"

Someone whom never left my side-
And comforts me like no other,
A friend that I can depend on-
Who's closer to me than my brother.
When in trouble, I call his name-
He hears me when I cry,
He comforts me and wipe away my tears-
Falling from my eye.
He's always there for when I call-
In truth I can depend,
Christ is this friend, that I depend-
To you, I recommend.
He is a friend that's always there-
He's closer than a brother,
He's there to meet thy deepest needs-
To comfort, like no other.

By: Terry Webb

"THANKS FOR GIVING"

Not for the food, you have to eat,
Nor for the animals, that give you meat.
But for His life, that set you free,
On that special day, at Calvary.
The way into Heaven, could not be bought,
But the death of Jesus, redemption was wrought.
So thank him for the life he gave,
His life for yours, His blood did save.
Thank him for the life you're living,
The life He gave, Thank Him for giving.

By: Terry Webb

"THE LAMB WHO DIED"

He shed His blood then gave His life
All this at Calvary,
He did this all to save mankind
From sin to set man free.

He was the ultimate sacrifice
Christ the Lamb who died,
His blood was shed for all mankind
Now we're justified.

It's by His own atoning blood that
We have been made whole,
And by the name of Jesus Christ
Brings joy unto my soul.

By: Terry Webb

"THE ULTIMATE SACRAFICE"

The Lord, whom formed the world by word
The moon, the stars, the sky,
He left His glorious home above
To come to earth and die.

He left His Holy Throne on high
To enter time and space,
So he could meet our deepest need
That need of ours was grace.

He was willing to suffer affliction
To suffer even loss,
By becoming the ultimate sacrifice
And die upon a cross.

How precious is our Savior's blood
That makes us white as snow,
He gave His life on Calvary
His blood from him did flow.

He took the place of all mankind
He faced the world alone,
He became the ultimate sacrifice
Our sins He did atone.

By: Terry Webb

"SILENT SOUNDS"

Silent sounds all around, listen, can you hear?
The silent sounds of taps, saying Jesus is near.
He's tapping at your heart, for you to let him in,
He wants to be your Savior, companion and your friend.

Shhh, be quiet, is that him at your door?
If it's Him rejoice, do not worry anymore.
So listen, get ready, His taps are getting near,
Open up your heart to him, you will clearly hear.

By: Terry Webb

"OPEN THE DOOR"

Our behavior must be beyond reproach
Integrity is the key,
That opens the door to our spiritual life
Victorious we will be.

Open the door, your hearts made pure
God's grace to magnify,
His word of life, to all make known
God alone glorifies.

By: Terry Webb

"GOD, THE OMNIPOTENT"

In times you feel you're all alone
Know that someone's there,
Know that God the Omnipotent one
Is with you everywhere.

He's with you everywhere you go
He see's all things you do,
Know that God, the Omnipotent one
is always there with you.

By: Terry Webb

"GOD'S ETERNAL WILL"

We try and try to live our lives
The best way as we can,
But we don't live accordingly
To God's eternal plan.

We need the Lord within our lives
His purpose to fulfill,
There is no other way to life
Than God's eternal will.

By: Terry Webb

"GOD'S GREATNEST"

The attributes of God are seen
In everything we see,
Being understood by the things He made
The forest, the sky and sea.
All living creatures, great and small
Reveal His love and care,
The greatness of our God is seen
In all things everywhere.

By: Terry Webb

"GOD, OUR REFUGE"

God is our refuge and our strength
our help when tempest roll,
That we may find peace, and quiet within
to the utmost of our soul.

Our trust should be in God alone
Always and forever,
For he is faithful unto the end
Never changing, ever!

By: Terry Webb

"GOD'S UNFAILING LOVE"

I trust in God, I know he care,
On top the mountain, I know He's there.
For in the rise, though billows may roll,
He will protect, and keep my soul.

When I look out, It may be night,
But when I look up, it's always light.
Across the rough, and stormy sea,
God's unfailing love, comforts me.

By: Terry Webb

"WHY PRAY?"

You may not like the circumstance–
In which you face each day,
Think of why you face those things–
My friend you do not pray!

The grip of habit, can be strong–
In sin, your eyes can dim,
You, who've known and loved the lord–
Will lose all sense of him.

Prayer brings peace, and gives us power–
To walk the Christian way,
Prayer links us to the living God–
That's why we need to pray!

By: Terry Webb

"GIVING"

Everything that you give in life
Should be without a measure,
For when you give, give out of love
That gift will then be treasure.

Your sacrifice, touched with your love
Such joy that gift will bring,
Someone may smile, or maybe laugh
But their hearts will surely sing.

By: Terry Webb

"GOD OUR STRENGTH"

God of love, Our Father in Heaven
Thou whom dwell's in light,
We lean on thee and all Thy love
And rest upon Thy might.

For even in our weakness, Lord
Our joy will still abound,
In Thee "O" Lord we are made strong
Our strength in Thee is found.

By: Terry Webb

"GOD'S PARDON"

Consider what the Lord has done
He came down from above,
To offer pardon and peace to all
By sacrifice of love.

By him the world has overcome
With power over sin,
For he has paid the penalty
Of sin that lurks within.

For by His own atoning blood
Spilled on Calvary,
Our sins are now washed away,
Purged, we are set free.

By: Terry Webb

"TRUE WITNESS"

I pray for wisdom, "O" Lord my God
From you, my God above,
For with this wisdom that I'll receive
I'll share my Saviors love.

I want to be a true witness Lord
And profess your Holy word,
To go where some have never been
For some have never heard.

So grant me Lord, this one request
And Help me persevere,
To spread Thy Word, where I may go
And make it loud and clear.

By: Terry Webb

"THE CHILDREN"

We must teach the children teaching of
Christ to our daughters and sons,
We must speak the truth to our
Precious little one's.

We must teach the children that there
Is one whom loves them more,
Of one who loves them more than you
now and forever more.

And we must teach our children
To beware of Satan too,
And we must teach our children
Trust in God their life time through.

By: Terry Webb

"THE LORD I TRUST"

"O" Lord, in you alone I trust-
To keep me from alarm,
In tangled paths of life I know-
You'll save me from all harm.

You'll keep me always in Thine eye-
That I'll not go astray,
Like sheep that sometimes wander off-
And often lose their way.

In you alone I trust "O" Lord-
To guide my steps always,
Upon a path of righteousness-
That leads to brighter day's.

By: Terry Webb

"POWER OF THE RIGHTEOUS"

The power of the righteous
Shall reign in the end,
It shall conquer over evil workers
Living lives of sin.
Jesus is this righteous power
Behold, all eyes will see,
The day He comes for His elect
Forever to be free.

By: Terry Webb

"SERVING GOD"

There is joy in serving God
And walking in His light,
For I have learned this wondrous thing
To do what's true and right.

If we just do what's true and right
And serve God everyday,
We need not have to fear at all
What others have to say.

The Lord, He came to show this world
On how each one must live,
He taught us all, how we must love
And how to share and give.

So there is joy in serving God
Whom died within our place,
He showed a dying world His love
And magnified His grace.

By: Terry Webb

"JOY OF THE LORD"

Within God is the fountain of life–
Through him shall we see light,
His righteousness to the upright in heart–
His love is ever bright.

Excellent is his loving-kindness to man–
There is peace under his wing,
I find fulfilling joy in the Lord–
And praise to him I sing.

Within God's presence is fullness and joy–
Comfort is in his love,
Pleasures evermore in the joy of the Lord–
You'll find in God above.

By: Terry Webb

"GOD'S MYSTERIOUS WAYS"

No one knows the ways of God
No one knows his plan,
His ways are very mysterious to man
No one can understand.

Never will we know why God's
Blessings ever flow,
Even for the sinful man
No one will ever know.

By: Terry Webb

"LOVE WITHOUT END"

A special love, unto all men,
God has given, deep within.
He gave his only begotten son,
The battle of sin, is now won.

His precious son, Jesus Christ,
Gave his life, for this price.
This was love, for God to send,
His son to man, Love without end!

By: Terry Webb

"PRAY"

Come my child to my throne of grace
Your needs to me make known,
Bring to me child, your daily burdens
Never carry them alone.

Let your requests be known to me
I will take the clouds away,
I then will let my blessings flow
If you take time to pray.

By: Terry Webb

"LIGHT OF THE WORLD"

You can enjoy who you are
Dispelled from the night,
In a world filled with darkness
Jesus is the light.
The prince of peace who promised
To light the very way,
Who let's you know you're safe
In the unknown world today.

"I am the light of the world
Those who follow me,
Will never be in darkness
And surely be set free."
Mighty God, everlasting father
Glorious God of Love,
Jesus is the light of the world
In Heaven high above.

By: Terry Webb

"MAJESTY OVER ALL"

He is supreme, Majesty over all,
The rich, the great, the poor, the small.
Over the young, and over the old,
His heart is love, with the richness of gold.
No one is greater, than his Majesty,
His glory is far, beyond the eye can see.
Angels in Heaven, bow to him and sing,
For He is Lord and Majesty, over everything.

By: Terry Webb

"JESUS IS WAITING"

Each man that lives, in him there is sin,
And he will be judged, when this world end.
But Jesus awaits, with an extended hand,
To forgive all sin, in each and every man.

The poor, the rich, the great and the small,
He's just waiting, for each one to call.
He only just ask, two things from men,
One is to repent, to him their sin.

The other is to live, for Him each day,
Be Christ like to others, go to Church and pray.
It's not so much, that He ask you to do,
And remember, "Jesus is waiting on you."

By: Terry Webb

"THINK"

Take a moment to stop and think
The light you then shall see,
The grace the Lord bestowed on you
From sin to set you free.

Stop and think of all your blessings
How trials have lost their sting,
Then think about Christ's love for you
Your heart will surely sing.

By: Terry Webb

"UNDER HIS WINGS"

Under his wings, I am safe always
My life, He doth guard well,
Though I walk the valley of shadow and death
I fear no evil or Hell.
Within this world the nights may deepen
The tempest games are wild,
Under God's wings I am safely abiding
My God, and I, His child.

By: Terry Webb

"THE CHAIN'S OF SIN"

Linked together, hands and feet
Your life a chain of sin,
For all have sinned against the Lord
Sin is in all men.
Christ gave his life to save this world
His life was for our sin,
He broke the chains of sin and death
now we must change within.

By: Terry Webb

"PLEASE GRANT ME"

Lord grant me wisdom, that I should know,
Please grant me love, that overflow.
Lord grant me joy, within my heart,
Please forgive my sins, for a brand new start.
Lord grant me sight, so that I may see,
The road that you, have prepared for me.
Lord grant me peace, and serenity,
Please grant me life, happy and free.

By: Terry Webb

"SERVE THE LORD"

He is the Alpha and the Omega–
Forever He's the same,
Christ, He is the life to all–
Proclaim His Holy Name.

Serve the Lord with gladness–
Cut a different mold,
Be now of the Lord's concern–
To reap your crown of gold.

By: Terry Webb

"KEEP IN STEP"

Keeping in step with the Savior
Just walk the Christian way,
Will He not then care for you?
His word you will obey.
Pray to Him, give Him your heart
Live a life that's true,
Then Christ the Lord will satisfy
And prove what Grace can do!

By: Terry Webb

"GIVE ME PEACE"

Peace of mind is all I want
But peace is hard to find,
We're told to bless our enemies
Yet they are still unkind.

God is in control, I know
I need not doubt or fear,
Though my enemies rise against me,
God is always near.

The mighty hand of God will move
To wipe them all away,
Then the righteous, shall have peace
Forever and a day.

By: Terry Webb

"LOVING THE LORD"

You must walk each step, in the Lords way,
Step, step, step after step, day after day.
Surely you must know, to be obedient and true,
That will reflect the love, of the Lord in you.
You must Love the Lord, more than anyone,
For He is your Savior, God's begotten Son.
You must love the Lord, more than anything,
He is much greater, than a President or King.
So give your heart to Him, Jesus high above,
Your deepest and utmost, sincere feelings of love.

By: Terry Webb

"MY AMAZING LOVE"

My amazing love, how can it be,
That you "O" Lord, has died for me?
How can it be, that I should gain,
From your blood, and all your pain?
Yet you "O" Lord, died on the cross,
For all my sins, cause I was lost.
He died for me, and also for you,
He rose again, the third day too.
He gave His life, that we should gain,
Eternal life, through all his pain.
My amazing love, our mediator,
To our father God, the creator.
My amazing love, whom died for sin,
For redemption between, God and men.

By: Terry Webb

"NEVER ALONE"

Never do we share alone-
Our worries nor our cares,
Jesus says he's there with you-
Your problems he will share.
He's always there beside us-
We're never left alone,
He's there to guide and comfort-
He looks out for his own.
Never do we share alone-
One moment of our day,
Jesus will be there with you-
Every step of the way . . .

By: Terry Webb

"HELP ME LORD"

Help me Lord to be not afraid
Of things not yet to come,
Also to place my trust in you
More to say than some.
Help me also to be afraid "O" Lord
Of disobeying you,
I need your help "O" Lord my God
In everything I do.

By: Terry Webb

"TO HEAVEN, BY LOVE"

He loves me and he let's me know,
Each day for him, my love does grow.
He gave his life, for me he died,
Christ, my Lord was crucified.
He taught me how, my life should be,
Christ the Lord, whom died for me.
With him, my life is edified,
Because his word, in me abide.
He is to me, my all in all,
He lifts me up, at times I fall.
He washed all, my sins away,
And will come back, for me one day.
Heaven then, I will come in,
For he has washed away my sin.
Heavens gate will open wide,
And there with him, I will abide.
Forever, with my Lord above,
Because he gave, to me his love.

By: Terry Webb

"THE BRIDGE OF GRACE"

The hands of God are reaching out
He is the bridge of grace,
Each day he sends His loving aid
For trials in which we face.
Lift up thine eyes and seek His face
The one whom cares for thee,
Run straight the race, in faith thru grace
Then cross this bridge with me.

By: Terry Webb

"THE LOVE OF GOD"

We do not know the mind of God
But His love He has made known,
For through His love He gave His son
That we may be His own.

We know not why His wondrous grace
Extends to sinful man,
Nor why He chose the sinful man
To fit into His plan.

We know not why His love for us
Is beyond the stars above,
But we should be more than grateful
God extends to man His love.

By: Terry Webb

"PLAN AHEAD"

The Bible says to worry not–
About the things of tomorrow,
Our lives are but a gift from God–
Our times are just on borrow.

But we must plan ahead in life–
On where our soul will go,
But where our soul will go my friend–
Is only for God to know.

But always think ahead in life–
Of blessings yet to be,
Your life must be both true and right–
For life eternally.

How glorious it is to think ahead–
On where your soul will go,
With help from God, while life shall last–
Your future you shall know.

By: Terry Webb

"PRINCE OF PEACE"

For unto us the Lord He came
And took the form of man,
He came to all as Prince of peace
Revealing to us God's plan.

Upon our lives shed forth his grace
With Him, mercy mild,
All glory to the Prince of peace
God and sinners, reconciled.

By: Terry Webb

"SEEK THE LORD"

Seek the Lord and you will find,
Love, joy and peace of mind.
Seek the Lord and you will see,
Just how his love can truly be.

Return to him, the redeemer of you,
He loved you so He died for you.
The Lord is not that far away,
He's with you now, and everyday.

Faith is the answer, knowing He's there,
And always is, because he care.
Seek Him now, and you will find,
His love for you, is one of a kind.

By: Terry Webb

"PRAYER"

"Dear Heavenly Father, I come before
Your most Holy Throne of grace,
Asking you to help me be more gracious
To others as you have been to me.

By: Terry Webb

"GOD WILL CALL US ALL"

A road in which is hard to walk-
But the best there is to trod,
Blessed is this road for all-
The one that leads to God.

There is no need for worry-
Because God, He walks ahead,
But some has turned the other way-
Away from God instead.

God will call us all one day-
And take us by the hand,
To lead us into a paradise-
His own chosen land.

Nothing you will ever want-
He will be your hearts desire,
Those who turned away from Him-
Will meet in hell bound fire.

God will call us all one day-
Then our eyes will see,
The Glory of our Lord and Savior-
Lord and majesty.

He will take us to a paradise-
His home so beautiful,
And we will live forever there-
A life so wonderful.

God will call us all one day-
Like a Sheppard with his fold,
He will lead the strong and weak-
The weary and the old.

God will call us all one day-
But only for the blest,
They'll receive the crown of life-
An be given Heavenly rest.

By: Terry Webb

"O" LORD WHY?

My child, my child, I don't understand why?
Tell me why did my child, have to die.
Why did my child, have to leave me?
Why does death, exist to be?

I don't know why, my child had to go,
Please tell me Lord why, so I will know.
Then I came to realize, we were born to die,
So when death comes, don't worry or cry.

They're no longer living in this world of sin,
But in the arms of Jesus, living again.
So take away my tear "O" Lord from my eye,
I now know, why my child had to die.

By: Terry Webb

"LIKE SHEEP"

Like sheep we seek to find His love
We search and it is found,
Like sheep we need to hear His voice
Oh, what a joyful sound.

Like sheep that sometimes wander off
And often lose their way,
Like sheep we need God's watchful eye
To keep us day by day.

By: Terry Webb

"MY PRAYER HEARD"

I was dumb with silence, I held my peace–
Even my sorrow was stirred,
My heart was hot, it burned within me–
But my prayer was heard.

"O" Lord, my God, make haste to help me–
Spare me part of the pain,
Hear my prayer give ear to my cry–
Please let Thy peace remain.

I waited patiently, for the Lord–
He inclined His ear to me,
He heard my cry and brought me up–
The Lord has set me free.

By: Terry Webb

"THE WEEPING SHEEP"

Man is like sheep, in the lord's eye
He protects and watch over them,
And comforts them when they cry
His sheep is very precious to him.

If like sheep, man get lost
from the Church he strays away,
Lost sheep will cry for their Sheppard
But to the Lord man will pray.

On the cross the Lord bought the right
To save all who were lost,
He gave his life, the pain he endured
Surely Jesus paid the cost.

By: Terry Webb

"HIS LIFE WAS FOR ME"

My savior died, his life was for me,
He gave His life, that I may be free.
His blood was to wash, away my sin,
I now have communion, with his father again.
For me, like the world, we're destined to die,
Corrupt with sin, in the sight of God's eye.
Jesus gave His life, truly an act of love,
To give us life in Him, in paradise above.
He gave His life, for all to be free,
He shed His blood, His life was for me.

By: Terry Webb

"THY WILL"

Take my hand and guide me Lord
Lead my feet and heart,
So from Thy will I will not stray
Nor from Thy truth depart.

Keep me in Thy truth dear Lord
Thy precepts to obey,
Lest unbelief of heart "O" Lord
Cause my feet to stray.

Not my will, but your will Lord
Let Thy spirit dwell,
Within my heart so all can see
My face will clearly tell.

By: Terry Webb

"THE BLOOD OF JESUS"

How precious is the saviors blood
For sin His blood did flow,
Just one drop of His precious blood
Will cleanse thee white as snow.

Nothing but the blood of Christ
For sin it was required,
Christ's sacrifice is exactly what
God almighty desired.

By: Terry Webb

"THE NAME OF JESUS"

The name Jesus, is such a beautiful name
A name I love to hear,
A name that's known by everyone
This name is very dear.
A name that means Salvation
To a dying human race,
A name that means victory
And a name that means grace.
This name is known throughout the world
This name will set you free,
If you call upon this name for help
He saves, for He saved me.

By: Terry Webb

"REACH OUT FOR LIFE"

As a flower opens up, to the break of day,
Man is the same, when he open his heart to pray.
Flowers seem to reach, for the glory of the sun,
Man is the same, when he reach for Christ, God's Son.
Beautiful is the flower, in it's full bloom,
Man is the same, in harmony with God's tune.
A flower reaches out, for life no doubt,
Man should do the same, for life reach out!

By: Terry Webb

"REACH OUT WITH LOVE"

To those who are in desperate need
And caught in life's despair,
Do for them what Jesus did–
Show them that you care.
With hands of love reach out to them
Reach out in Jesus name,
The love you give, will soon come back
More or just the same.

By: Terry Webb

"SAFE WITH THEE"

I lift my eyes to thee "O" Lord
My eyes so turned toward thee,
Steadfast and sure while billows roll
Thou art a rock for me.

I am confident that you will save me Lord
Your love always prevails,
For you alone is my inner strength
Your love for me never fails.

You have directed my path in every way
Your presence is ever near,
You are my light and my salvation Lord
So whom shall I fear?

Thou art an anchor for my soul
Kept in Thine hand above,
Thou art my hiding place and shield
I'm safe within Thy love.

By: Terry Webb

"GOD IS IN CHARGE"

Sometimes we lose control,
But God has a plan–
God He hasn't lost control,
He works in every man,
So let Him work His works in you,
He'll make your paths straight–
In all your ways acknowledge Him,
Just cooperate,
God is in charge so trust in Him,
For He will see you through–
God is in charge forevermore,
of both me and you!

By: Terry Webb

"LIKE YOU"

I want to be, as you are Lord
Your likeness, shining in me,
Your words, also Your deeds "O" Lord"
My heart, Your place to be.
Cleanse me of all secret faults
Then bring me to Your side,
Help me Lord to live my life
In Your grace I shall abide.
So help me be, as you are Lord
In all things that I do,
Help me to be, as you are Lord
I want to be like you.

By: Terry Webb

"MY SHIELD"

I have no need to worry, or have no need to fear,
The Lord is forever with me, and forever near.
For He will meet all my needs, He also will protect,
He has become my personal shield, His saved child elect.
I have no need to worry, on this battle field,
Jesus Christ, He alone, is my protecting shield.

By: Terry Webb

"I GIVE THANKS"

Thank you Lord, for Your foundation,
Providing me, with my salvation.
Thank You for, Your indwelling power,
Your spirit lives, in me this hour.

Thank You for, Your redeeming grace,
Joy and love, enlights my face.
Thank You Lord, my help today,
Thank You Lord, to you I pray.

By: Terry Webb

"HIS LOVE FOUND"

Every where you go, everywhere around–
you will find Jesus, His love can be found,
There's no place, that He is not there–
You'll find His presence, everywhere.

All around the world, every where you go–
You'll find that His love, will also flow,
Within each man, within his loving heart–
His love was born, right from the very start.

By: Terry Webb

"WHERE IS THE LOVE"

Where is the love God said to have—
To not put His name to shame?
Where is the brotherly love He said—
To have in Jesus name?

Where is the love that never fails—
To leave thy neighbor blessed?
Where is the love, that precious love—
That leaves the crowd impressed?

Where is the love, that tender love—
That comes through God, His power?
Where is that Godly love we need—
Each day and every hour?

To love thy neighbor as thy self—
This law is God's above,
You, who've known and loved the Lord—
Where now, is your love?

By: Terry Webb

"THY PERFECT LIGHT"

On Thy truth I've lived my life–
Thy Word has been my guide,
Thy Word has taught me what is wrong–
With sin I try to hide.

Thy perfect light has led my way–
Thy Word Lord is my sight,
I trust in You to lead my life–
Within Thy perfect light.

By: Terry Webb

"THE ARMOR OF GOD"

How awesome is Thy power Lord,
Thou belt of truth and piercing sword.
To all you men, in every nation,
Take up thy helmet, of salvation.
The breastplate of righteousness, all in place,
You're ready for battle, face to face.
Prepare thy selves for the battle field,
In the gospel of peace, behind faiths shield.

By: Terry Webb

"THE RIGHT PATH"

Be careful of the path you choose
To life, do not choose wrong,
But let God's spirit, lead the way
Your habits, may be strong.
Come now while the Savior is calling
And enter into His gate,
Leave the path where fools have trod
Tomorrow may be too late.

By: Terry Webb

"STRONG HANDS"

Double hands will hold, on a promise I depend,
My destiny and soul, He will keep till the end.
In His care securely, with Gods eternal grip,
With strong hands that hold, if I ever slip.

In strong hands of God, I am held secure,
With divine finality, Gods hands are sure.
I will never perish, in His hands securely,
Held by strong hands, in count for eternity.

By: Terry Webb

"LIVING FOR GOD'S GLORY"

What ever you do, in this world today,
You must thank the Lord, with words that say.
Glory, Praise and honor to Him,
You need to do, what glorifies Him.
Whatever you say, and whatever you do,
Must show the glory, of God in you.

By: Terry Webb

"MY STRENGTH, THE LORD"

I pray and ask for strength, to get all duties done,
Then I pray and thank the Lord, God's precious Son.
For He and only He, has made possible the way,
So I praise the Lord for my strength, each and every day.
For He is to me my strength, He also is my light,
He make all things, for me alright.

By: Terry Webb

"I LOVE YOU JESUS"

My love, and true love, Jesus is to me,
He's everything and more, in Him I am free.
He woke me this morn, at the break of day,
He keeps my mind on Him, and reminds me to pray.
He protects me through the day, in case I stumble or fall,
For He knows the way, He's been through it all.
At the end of each day, He calls me in for the night,
For you must walk in the day, for then you're in the light.
The time is then come, for me to rest, my head,
My Jesus, still with me, He tucks me into bed.
This is why my Jesus, is my one and only Love,
My only true love, from Heaven high above.

By: Terry Webb

"HIS NAME ABOVE ALL"

There is a name more greater than any,

The rich, the famous, the greatest of many.

His name means Salvation, for He past the test,

His name is Glorified, for He is the best.

His name is known throughout all the land.

His name means Savior, to every woman and man,

His name is manifested, even in the Heavens above,

In both Heaven and earth, His name means Love.

His name is JESUS, LORD, SAVIOR, and KING,

Even the Angels in Heaven, bow to Him and sing.

By: Terry Webb

"WHAT I KNOW FOR SURE"

What I know for sure, it is never God's intention,
To abandon us in life, in any situation.
What I know for sure, is that the goal in which He aims-
He promise future deliverance, my redeemer proclaim.

What I know for sure, is that when He makes a promise-
He always keep His word, with Him you'll never miss.
What I know for sure, is that within a special way,
That because of His Victory, Victory is mine today!

By: Terry Webb

"THROUGH FAITH"

A living faith is a working faith
So let our lives express,
Let's follow Christ in all He did
His Word we must profess.

We are saved by grace, through faith
Our works and virtues shine,
So let us love in deed and truth
To prove Christ is divine.

By: Terry Webb

"THE GOODNESS OF YOU"

Each morn I awake, with the risen sun
My heart in Christian love,
My soul is happy in Jesus, my Lord
Christ whom reigns above.

God's goodness, all His strength and love
I found within His Son,
The joy of life with all it's goodness
I found in the Living One!

The goodness of you, "O" Lord, my God
My life you made anew,
Each day I wake, I start my day
In the goodness of You . . .

By: Terry Webb

"THE ROAD AHEAD"

Are you prepared to travel my friend,
Down the narrow road ahead?
Or will you keep on going backward,
On the destructive road instead?
Come and follow Me my friend,
The Lord Jesus is the way–
Come let's walk this road together,
Let's walk this road today.

By: Terry Webb

"GLORY TO GOD"

Glory to God, He is the most high,
In the Heavens above, and below the sky.
Wonderful Savior is He, "Thou Majesty,"
All power and glory, belong to Thee.

The Angels worship Him, our Lord and King,
Songs of praises, to Him, they sing.
Only God, taketh the sin from man,
"Only God," truly understand.

"Only God," gives life to you and me,
Yes, "Only God," abundantly.
God is life, God is also love,
Glory to God, in Heavens above.

By: Terry Webb

"LIVING IN LOVE"

As the Father love me, so I have loved you
Now remain in my love,
My joy may constantly prevail your life
Blessings from high above.
I tell you now live, in that sphere of perfect love
and then as you obey;
You will continue to live in that perfect love
In God's commandments, everyday!

By: Terry Webb

"MY WALK WITH GOD"

Early one morning, I rubbed my drowsy head-
Giving thanks to God, I jumping out of bed,
That same day, I ran into my God-
While walking, the very road I trod,

Over beyond my side, He was standing there-
Then I looked around, He was every where,
Surprisingly amazed, it turned out to be-
I was walking with my God, inside of me.

By: Terry Webb

"HIS SPIRIT LIVES"

The love of God within our hearts
Let others clearly see,
The radiant power of the Lord
Whom died at Calvary.

Within our heart's His spirit lives
For In our hearts do dwell,
His Holy Spirit and all can see
Our faces clearly tell.

By: Terry Webb

"WHO IS GOD?"

Who would say, there is no God?
Their minds, bodies and feet not shod!
What man would stand against God and revile?
Does he not know, his life is on trial?

They think that God does not exist;
They think that God is just a mist.
"Who is God?" unbelievers would say,
"Show me God," then I might pray.

In truth I tell you, He is a living God,
Believe in Him, and keep thy feet shod.
In the gospel of peace, truth, and of love,
Soon you'll meet, this awesome God above.

By: Terry Webb

"PRAYER 2"

Dear Lord in Heaven, you know my deepest needs of
You and your strength. Please open my mind to your
instruction and empower me in your love each day.
In Jesus name I pray . . . . Amen

By: Terry Webb

"YOU CAN DEPEND"

You can depend on God, He will always care,
His tender loving mercy, flows every where.
You can depend on Him, He will not pass you by,
He's forever watchful, from Heaven above so high.
You can depend him, if you are God's child,
He will comfort you, all your life long while.
You can depend him, God Almighty is true,
Everlasting, is His love for you.

By: Terry Webb

"THOU ART GREAT"

How great Thou art, who made the sky,
And reigns in Heaven, above so high.
Thy loving hands, are always there,
Your forgiving heart shows that you care.
With mercy always in Thine eye,
A special love I can't deny.
Every man, woman, and even child,
Thine heart is open with a smile.
How great Thou art who has so much,
Power and such a gentle touch.
Thou knowest the heart of every man,
And everyone, You understand.
Thou shinest a light upon each day,
To help guide man along his way.
So much power, so much love,
Combined in one great Lord above.
With a tender, loving, forgiving heart,
Jesus Christ, HOW GREAT THOU ART!

By: Terry Webb

"WHAT MORE"

He left His Father's throne above–
To save the human race,
He emptied all Himself, but love–
So full, was His grace.

He died in place of all mankind–
What more can He now do,
The price of sin, His life has paid–
He did this just for you.

By: Terry Webb

"TEACH YOUR CHILD"

Teach your child, in the ways of God
And they will never stray,
Teach them how to trust in Him
To worship Him and pray.

Teach them all, to know their God
To render Him control,
Teach them, they must give to Him
Their mind, heart, and soul.

By: Terry Webb

"THE SPIRIT OF GRACE"

The Son of God, is the spirit of grace,
He died to save, the human race.
"The Lord will judge, and He will repay"
All His people, on judgment day.
Be careful in life, don't sinfully trod,
For one day you'll answer, to the Living God.
For who has insulted, the spirit of Grace?
Woe to him, when the Lord shows His face.
For the Lord will come, and He will not tarry,
Only those in faith, away He will carry.
He who has trampled, on the spirit of Grace,
Will be destroyed, from the human race!

By: Terry Webb

"SPIRITUALLY CLEAN"

Search me Lord deep down within
Know my heart today,
Try me Lord and know my thoughts
This to You I pray.

Please see if there be wickedness
Deep down within me,
Then cleanse me Lord of every sin
O Lord, set me free.

By: Terry Webb

"NO OTHER GOD"

He is the first and the last
There is no other God,
He is the creator of all things
In this life you trod.

You can't be saved by no one else
But by Jesus, God's only Son,
Under heaven, there has been given to man
No other God, but one.
"JESUS"

By: Terry Webb

"ONLY YOU LORD"

Only You Lord, know the stain of sin I bear,
And I must release my guilt, to Your loving care.
Only You Lord, gave Your life to save me,
With every passing moment, I give my life to Thee.

Only You Lord, the one to which I praise,
Only You Lord, holds everlasting days.
Only You Lord, has lifted me from shame,
Only You Lord, I give praise to your name.

By: Terry Webb

"GOD? OR NOT?"

Scientist say there is no God
They teach this now in school,
Evolution explains the mystery of life
Oh how they are the fool.
With wisdom, God created the planets
Unchained, but yet in place,
With wisdom, God created mankind
Like spiders weaving their lace.
How awesome are the works of God
He is all wise and true,
Scientist may say He doesn't exist
But I believe he do.

By: Terry Webb

"LOVE HIM"

Love Him whom the world dislikes
Receive Him, Heaven has won,
Rejecting Him, will lead to hell
Because Christ, is God's Son.

Believe in Him, the Son of God
By His grace we now are blest,
Render all thy praise to Him
To enter into His rest.

By: Terry Webb

"SON'S OF GOD"

God chastens those that are his son's
When they begin to stray,
He lifts his chastening hand in love
To help them see his way.

He will ever keep their souls from harm
For he know what's in their heart,
His love for them will never end
Nor ever will it part.

By: Terry Webb

"WE HAVE A CHANCE"

There's a chance for all to live
In peace and harmony,
This chance that we all have
To be forever free.
This chance that we all have
It's price is already paid,
To eternal life in paradise
The road is already made.
This chance is for everyone
Yes everyone that live,
Paid by the blood of the lamb
Christ the one that give.
He gave his life and his blood
That we be cleansed of sin,
He only ask that we repent
And be a light to men.
Take hold to this chance my friend
It may be your last,
Repent and live for Jesus Christ
Away from sins past.

By: Terry Webb

"WHITER THAT SNOW"

When God redeems a sinner
With the atoning blood of his son,
Not one stain of their sins remains
Therefore, the sinner is won.

The wonderful power in the blood of Christ
Redeems with life giving flow,
The stain of sin through Christ is lost
much whiter now than snow.

By: Terry Webb

"WHY WORRY"

Why do God's children worry so–
Does He not care for them?
Does He not love and cherish those–
Who praise and worship Him?

Do they not know that in His love–
He keeps them from alarm?
And through His love He keeps them safe–
Protected from all harm.

The love of God makes them secure–
Through all that do betide,
His children will never be in want–
For them God will provide.

So why do His children worry so?
For God is in control,
Though trouble assail, and dangers fright–
God will save their soul . . .

By: Terry Webb

"THROUGH EYES OF LOVE"

The kindness of love, don't focus on faults,
But it sees beyond, with a love result.
Looking past qualities, of only the good,
God helps us see, a love we should.

Through eyes of love, love is never blind,
It's an inner vision, that's quick to find.
The beauties and qualities, held from common sight,
Through eyes of love, bring an added light.

By: Terry Webb

"PRAYER 3"

Please help me Lord, to walk Thy way
And surrender my love to You today,
Oh Lord, my God, in Heaven above
Let me surrender my heart, unto your love.

By: Terry Webb

"THE ROYAL LAW"

Owe no man nothing
But love one another,
Therefore love your neighbor
As thyself as a brother.

To fulfill the laws of God
He strictly demand,
Remember His royal law's
Everything that He command.

Briefly comprehended
You must do what He say,
God's royal Law is the law
You must honor and obey.

By: Terry Webb

"RUILING PASSION"

Living for the Lord whom died
For sin He took my place,
Bearing on the cross my shame
And also my disgrace.

Such love He has for me a sinner
To answer when I call,
In return, to Him I give
To Him I give my ALL!

By: Terry Webb

"STRONG FAITH"

My faith is in the Lord above
Through Him the sun does shine,
Each day His hand directs my path
Hand in hand with mine.

Though darkened clouds above may be
I trust in Him each day,
Though mighty winds above may blow
My faith in God always.

By: Terry Webb

"NO GREATER LOVE"

Jesus gave His life, for both you and I,
On the cross at Calvary, He hung there to die.
In dying for this world, He showed the greatest love,
He was meek as a lamb, gentle as a dove.

He had the courage, to give his life for a friend,
To endure the pain and agony, till the bitter end.
Life is important, the most precious gift to man,
Man tries to hold on, as long as he can.

But Jesus gave it all, His life upon a cross,
That's how much He loves us all, He paid our cost!

By: Terry Webb

"GOD'S JOY"

No one knows the ways of God
His ways are yet unknown,
But under the Heavens skies above
His works are clearly shown.
This world is filled with so much good
It's also filled with pleasure.
God has filled our lives with joy
Above all earthly treasure.

By: Terry Webb

"GOD'S WORD"

Every word of God is pure
Keep them in thine heart,
God's word will help you in this life
Therefore, do not impart.
His word will be to you each day
Guardian and your guide,
The Word of God will always be
Forever by your side.

By: Terry Webb

"LOVE EACH OTHER"

Towards every man, there's one true friend,
He rends a love, that never end.
He gives His all, no fret or fuss,
The love He share, and gives to us.

Equally sharing, with every man,
A love no man, yet understand.
But yet to man, His solemn grace,
Love light shines, upon their face.

He tells each man, to be the same,
And live up to, His Holy name.
To share their love, each brotherly man,
The same as He, to fulfill His plan.

His plan will be, a new generation,
Of brotherly men, In a Godly nation.
Where every man, will be thy brother,
And every man, will love one another.

By: Terry Webb

"HOPE IN GOD"

The Lord our God the solid rock
His ways unwavering and sure,
Our hope must be in the Lord our God
Whom makes our hope secure.

He bought us with His precious blood
That day on Calvary,
That our faith and hope be him alone
For He has set us free.

Our hope is more than wishful thinking
Cause Jesus Christ still live,
God sent His son to give us hope
To cleanse us and forgive.

By: Terry Webb

"LIKE A CHILD"

Yearning for greatness, is a deadly human disease,
Men want to be wealthy, and do as they please.
Building up their treasures, on this planet earth,
When they die their treasure, to them have no worth.

Now a little child, without a single care,
Depend upon his parents, knowing they are there.
Without a single worry. in this dreaded world,
Every child is carefree, every boy and girl.

We must be like children, with a loving kind heart,
To enter Gods Kingdom, it's time we should start.
God is your Father, be humble in your love,
Be like a child, to get in heaven above.

By: Terry Webb

"TIME IS AT HAND"

Time is getting near, and it's almost at hand,
For the end of this world, and the judgment of man.
For this world has turned, for thousands of years,
And man has suffered, and shed many tears.

Because of sin, entering into mans heart,
This sin has caused, God and man to be apart.
Generations have past, getting closer to the end,
Yet sin still remains, in the hearts of all men.

Sin has led man, from the Godly road they once trod,
Sin has caused man, to be an abomination to God.
"Sin," is something that God cannot tolerate,
"Sin," is something that God truly hate.

For God made man, in the image of He,
In his own image, He has made thee.
God is good, but he cannot stand,
Sin in the heart, of his creation man.

And soon there will be, a final war,
A war of the God's, to even the score.
The Lord almighty, of good will win,
Sin no more, will be in the hearts of men.

For one day you'll see, coming from Heaven's sky,
A glorious sight, unto the human eye.
Be on guard, for the TIME IS AT HAND,
For the coming of the Lord, and the judgment of man!

By: Terry Webb

"TWO ROADS"

There are two roads, that you may trod,
One road is bad, the other leads to God.
Be careful in your choice, or you may loose,
The choice is yours, but you must choose.

There are two roads, which will you take?
Make your choice wise, in the decision you make.
To light up your path, along your journey way,
Ask God to guide you, each and every day.

Brothers and sisters, please choose the right one,
For the road you choose, must be with Gods son.
There are other roads, that will lead you astray,
With evil and destruction, along the way.

Which will you choose, which will you trod,
A road with evil, or a road with God!

By: Terry Webb

"THE CHOICE OF GOOD OR EVIL"

God first made, the Heavens and the earth,
He gave them both value, all their worth.
Then He made man, formed him from dust,
He formed this man, with the earth's crust.
This man was good with God, perfect as can be,
Had fellowship with God, totally sin free.
God told this man, of every tree you can eat,
But the tree of good and evil, you shall not eat.
Man was beguiled, and he ate fruit from this tree,
Immediately sin entered him, no longer he was free.
Man had followed evil, breaking God's command,
He disobeyed his Maker, God whom creating man.
He followed the path of evil, until this very day,
Then Jesus came teaching man, to repent and to pray.
Man has a choice, of doing what he should,
He still has the same choice, of evil or for good!

By: Terry Webb

"THE WAY TO SALVATION"

Jesus is the way, the way to salvation,
The way is Jesus, to Gods Holy nation.
Jesus said no one, will never truly see,
The paradise of Heaven, only but by Me.
The heart man believe, by mouth he shall confess,
Believe in Jesus Christ, Thou shall be blessed.
You shall be saved, by calling on His name,
The Holy name of Jesus, this name has no blame.
Jesus is the light, He is also the way,
Believe on Jesus Christ, believe in Him today.

By: Terry Webb

"THE LORD GIVETH AND TAKETH AWAY"

The Lord will give, and the Lord will take away,
If you are not true, to the Lord each day.
He may bless you, with everything you need,
Through His love for you, but please take heed.
The Lord is a jealous God, only Him you are to serve,
Don't turn your back on Him, You'll get what you deserve.
If you change directions, of roads along the way,
Your life will become bad, all things will fade away.
Be good to the Lord, and He will provide for you,
All He ask is serve Him, in all things you do.
Praise Him, be thankful, it's not hard if you try,
Except Him as your God, to see eye to eye.
He gives you blue skies, a sun to warm your face,
He placed the stars in Heaven, in their perspective place.
He gives for you the rain, which falls from the sky,
To keep alive all crop, for the sun has made dry.
But remember your life, that the Lord gives each day,
Don't be lost without Him, your life will fade away.

By: Terry Webb

"OUR ONLY HOPE"

God is the answer, and hope to everything–
We can find sanctuary, with our Heavenly King,
In sorrow or in sickness, He will see you through–
God's saving power, has healing in it too . . .

In tragedy or terror, you'll find Him there–
God's saving power, will follow everywhere,
Loneliness or whatever, God is the key–
He is our only hope, for you and for me.

By: Terry Webb

"HOW MANY YEARS WILL WE SHED TEARS?"

How much longer, will the world go on?
How much longer, will we linger on?
We have suffered ourselves, so many years,
Through wars, blood shed, and painful tears.
When God made man, He made man free,
He never intended, for wars to be.
We have now become, a dying human race,
Through wars and bloodshed, in this ungodly place.
"O" Lord My God, I wonder why?
Why do man, bring tears to the eye?
Man has been, is this world for so long,
And his heart continues, to lust for wrong.
Not thinking of, each precious little child,
That has to live, in this world for awhile.
Captivating each child, in an early start,
With violence imbedded, into their heart.
So many years, like the falling rain,
Man has endured, this hurting pain.
Brought upon himself, because he doesn't trod,
On the road and way, of our Creator God.

For man has chose wrong, to be his way,
That's why the world, is this way today.
We must learn, to live life right,
To the precious Lord, in His eye sight.
God gave Jesus, the power over all,
To conquer sin, man's down fall.
Man can live, his life and be free,
In the Lord Jesus, God intended us to be,
We can live under, His protective wing,
With no fears or worry, with new songs to sing.
But how much longer, will we suffer in tears?
Killing ourselves, in our dying years!

By: Terry Webb

"HOW LONG?"

How long will God tolerate, mans sinful ways?
How much longer, God giveth man days?
Seems that man has forgotten to follow Gods ways
How much longer, will God giveth man days?

To repent their sins, on bending knee
So Christ the Lord, may make them free
How long will man continue, living life wrong?
Ignoring Gods ways, tell me how long?

The reason Jesus Christ, has given His life
To make man whole, from suffering and strife
He gives man chance, all without demand
To know and obey, the words God command

How long will man, regretfully disobey
The Lord our God, the truth, the life and way?
How long will man, ignore salvation?
How long will man, live in this sinful nation?

How long will man, hold back his love
From the Lord Jesus, in the Heavens above?
How long, please tell me, how long and when
Will man prepare his soul, for the coming end?

By: Terry Webb

"THE ANGEL OF DEATH"

The angel of death, may come your way,
Anytime of night, or anytime of day.
He may come at any given hour,
And when he comes, "Death" is his power.
You cannot hide, nor can you run,
You can't escape death, Jesus was the only one.
And when death comes, you'll surely know,
Death will hit you with his fatal blow.
And when death hits, you'll surely cry,
Prepare yourselves, we are all destined to die.
So what can we do, what can be done?
Live for Jesus, God's only begotten son.
Repent good people, we are all reprobate,
Turn your sins to rend, before it's too late.
Don't let death find you, unclean and unsaved,
Before death sends you, to your fatal grave.
For it is written, that all men must die!
When death comes, you'll hear the cry.
Death always finds a place to go,
Deaths timing, you'll never know.
But Jesus, he paid deaths cost,
He gave his life, for all whom are lost.
Live for Jesus, and you will be saved,
After death, he opens your grave.
But remember, death may come, night or day,
And the angel of death, will come your way!

By: Terry Webb

"WHAT IS EASTER"

Easter is the day our Lord–
Rose from His short rest,
It is the day He resurrected–
A day in which is blest.

It is the day the Lord He proved–
Always to ever be,
That He is Lord and King of Kings–
For all eternity.

By: Terry Webb

"WHERE JESUS WALKED"

The road that Jesus walked, was a very rough road-
He asked no one for help, to carry up His load,
He walked along the sea, the Sea of Galilee-
He taught and fed five thousand, along beside that sea.

He walked through Bethlehem, the place where He was
born-
In a city called David, in a stable forlorn,
He walked in Capernaum, where He taught and He
preached-
In an ancient synagogue, His voice to people reached.

He walked in Old Jerusalem, He was greatly in demand-
Pilate resented Jesus, in words, "BEHOLD THE MAN"
He walked to Via Dolorosa, The way to the cross-
Dragging now His own cross, all seemed to be lost.

To the path of the skull, He journeyed through that way-
His life in human form, He gave it up that day,
Now He walks in Spirit, He walks with you and me-
Still guiding, also leading, to life eternally.

By: Terry Webb

"TELL ME ABOUT JESUS"

He was born in a manager, in a cradle of hay,
We celebrate this occasion now as Christmas Day.
He is the bright sunshine, full of glory,
Knowing He exist, you need not worry.
He is the light for you, also the light for me,
He is the light for all mankind, from sin we are set free.
. . . . TELL ME ABOUT JESUS . . . .
He is like the purity and kindness of a dove,
Our one and only Savior, sent from heaven above.
With a mighty voice, all our Savior Jesus has to do is speak,
He heals the blind, and give strength to the weak.
With Jesus Christ in your life, you are truly blessed,
Without Him in your life, you're living in distress.
. . . . TELL ME ABOUT JESUS . . . .
He strengthens you and he preserves you,
He will even fortify you.
He directs you and shelters you,
He will even help support you.
He is the help to all mankind,
If He had not come, we would still be blind.
He is God's son, earths Savior and King,
Who's precious gift of love, compares to other thing.
I can go on and on, with this never ending story,
but I will tell you this, He is my morning" Glory."

By: Terry Webb

"THE BIRTH OF CHRIST"

One day in manger, in a cradle of hay,
The Glory of the Lord, was delivered that day.
For Mary brought forth, her very first Son,
Wrapped in swaddling clothes, life has begun.
The angel of the Lord, had come upon them,
In the city of David, a city in Bethlehem.
For God in the highest, brought forth unto men,
His only begotten Son. to wash away sin.
People near and far, journeyed there to pray,
And see the Lord and Savior, who was born that day.

By: Terry Webb

"THE CRADLE"

That first Christmas, the Son of man came—
The Word was made flesh, Jesus was His name.
To think that God would choose, to enter human life—
Becoming a helpless baby, inside earthly strife.

Emptied of Heavens glory, so He could help you—
Now through the scriptures, He victoriously triumphed too.
With all that test us, He was tempted in every way—
When tested to the fullest, He was glorified that day.

Identifying Himself, with what's frail in you and me—
Sympathized our weakness, over all of it you see.
The Word was made flesh, Jesus was His name—
Born in a manger, The Son of man came!!!

By: Terry Webb

"THE DEATH OF CHRIST"

With no cause to die, Pilate had found in Thee,
He then washed His hands, to set you Lord free.
But instant loud voices, cried to him "Crucify"
Take Him to the cross, there let Him die.

The voices of them, and the chief priest prevailed,
Your death was required, attempts for freedom failed.
You were led to the skull, a place called Calvary,
They nailed you to a cross, they crucified Thee.

By: Terry Webb

"THE GOOD SHEPHERD"

The Lord Jesus Christ a very good shepherd
He truly loves His sheep,
His leads them to paths of righteousness
And comforts them when they weep.

Surely His sheep should fear no evil
For the Lord is always there,
The Lord Jesus Christ a very good shepherd
A shepherd that truly cares.

The Lord is my shepherd I shall not want
The Lord is good to me,
He is the shepherd who gave His life
To set His fold free.

By: Terry Webb

"THE HIGHEST GROUND"

Three wise men traveled far, to reach the highest ground,
They walked in faith with weary eyes,
their destination bound.
The night was calm and peaceful,
throughout the entire land,
These three men marched on and on,
through the desert sand.
Hope and joy filled their hearts, for whom
they journeyed to see,
Glory be to this guiding star, leading
their way shining brightly.
These three men came from very high grounds,
For they were three, royal wise kings.
They ended their journey at the highest grounds,
To worship Jesus, The King of Kings.

By: Terry Webb

"THE IMPORTANT STAR"

Tis a story, very old,
Sometimes said, or seldom told.
Which made for all, this Christmas day,
Let me tell you, if I may . . .

Long ago in Bethlehem, there was shown a light;
A distant star shining above, brightly in the night.
This star was very special, t'was different from the rest,
It's light guided all unto a stable that was blest.

This star it was important, it guiding through the night,
Leading all who came to see the glorious, wonderful sight.
This star led the way, for all who journeyed to see,
The precious little Savior, "Christ," the new born baby.

By: Terry Webb

"RESSURRECTION OF CHRIST"

On the third day, Mary Magdalene
Went to the place, Jesus last was seen
But only did she find, Jesus was not there
The grave where he lay, she found it was bare
Appeared were two angels, in the sepulture
Dressed in all white, they comforted her
They told Mary Magdalene, to run share and give
The news that Lord Jesus, yet again do live
From the dead our savior, Jesus Christ did rise
Appearing to His disciples, with them great surprise

By: Terry Webb

"SMILE FOR ME"

I looked up to the sky one day
And beheld a great surprise,
The Lord was looking down on me
From the heavens Glorious sky's.
I saw His face within a cloud
Then He smiled for me,
He said I'm with you always' child
Through all eternity.
You are to me my child elect
I'll keep you from alarm,
He said I'm with you always' child
To protect you from all harm.
From the heavens Glorious sky's above
The Lord looked down on me
He spoke to me from within a cloud
And then, "He smiled for me."
By: Terry Webb

"MOTHER IN LAW SPECIAL"

Your love to me is very special
You always seem to care,
No matter what we put you through
Your love was always there.

No matter what the circumstance
No matter what's been done,
You alway's called me son in law
And claimed me as your son.

No other love compares to yours
Except the Lord's above,
Mom you're alway's reaching out
To give your touch of love.

So I thank you mom for all your love
And all your vale of tears,
Your happy moments never dim
Through all your many years.

I love you and I always will
Cause you've been good to me,
One day you'll walk in paradise
Through all eternity.

By Terry Webb

"A MOTHER'S LOVE"

A mothers love is special
And important too,
A mothers love endures
Through all things you do.
It's something about that love
It always touch the heart,
And seems it's always there
As it was from the start.
A mother will take care
Of each precious little child,
And her love for them endures
All their life long while.
Mothers always know
For a mother knows best,
They seem to sense the trouble
Before you're put the test.
A mothers love is endless
And yet not fortold,
Because her love is pure
Her heart is made of gold.
Her love light brightly shine
Each day that she live,
For every precious child
Her heart will forgive.
Only the love of God
In Heaven high above,
Can over rule the heart
Of A Mothers Precious Love!

By Terry Webb

ABOUT THE AUTHOR

Terry Webb was born in Birmingham, Alabama on January 12, 1958 to Perry and Cora Mae Webb and came to Los Angeles, California at an early age. Terry graduated from high school in 1976 then he enlisted in the army to continue his education. Later he was Honorably Medically Discharged early from the Military due to a non-service related accident. Life was not the same for Terry after that. Although he found a job, the job didn't pay him enough to support his wife and son so he sold drugs on the side. The Money was good for a while but one day he was arrested and went to prison losing everything, including his wife and son. Upon the day of his parole, Terry tried desperately to put his life back together, but things for him were never the same. The streets of "Watts" became his hustle grounds and also his death trap because the drugs that he sold, he eventually became addicted to them himself.

After 15 years of struggling in his addiction, going back and forth to prison, sleeping in vacant houses, abandoned cars and on the side of freeways, digging out of trash cans for scraps, at his lowest point in life, Terry turned his life over to the care of God and asked the Lord Jesus into his heart. God has been in the midst of his deepest struggles and in time has restored everythingand more in Terry's life that was lost in his addiction.

Today, Terry is an active church member of the "CITY OF REFUGE" and "Mt CALVARY BAPTIST CHURCH" Terry doesn't do anything against the law but works with the law as a Loss Prevention Security Officer. God has also given Terry a heart of empathy and caring. With 4 years of study in Psychology and Chemical Dependency Counseling, he is also a Certified Substance Abuse Recovery Worker, Registered with the State of California.

Terry has become a professional helper and demonstrates his impulse to care by going over and beyond the expectations of his role in helping others. By the grace of God, his inspirational poems are to help others who are lost so that they may be found in Christ. Terry believes that "POETRY TO GOD" will change the lives of everyone who reads it, one person at a time, and will make the world a better place for everyone to live, one day at a time . . .

Look for all four Volumes Of
"POETRY TO GOD" online at:

Poetrytogod.org
Amazon.com
Barnes&noble.com

Poetry to God
Volume 1
Lord Please Hear the Cry

Poetry to God
Volume 2
No Fault Found

Poetry to God
Volume 3
Into Thine Hands

Poetry to God
Volume 4
**Prison Praise,
Cry's From Behind The Wall**

www.ingramcontent.com/pod-product-compliance
Lightning Source LLC
LaVergne TN
LVHW091254080426
835510LV00007B/262